{ UNDERSTANDING GRAMMAR }

NOUNS *and* PRONOUNS

ANN RIGGS

CREATIVE 🍎 EDUCATION

Published by Creative Education
P.O. Box 227, Mankato, Minnesota 56002
Creative Education is an imprint of The Creative Company
www.thecreativecompany.us

Design and production by Liddy Walseth
Art direction by Rita Marshall
Printed by Corporate Graphics in the United States of America

Photographs by Corbis (Stefano Bianchetti, Brooklyn Museum, Antar Dayal/Illustration Works,
Hulton-Deutsch Collection, Sylvain Sonnet), Corrie ten Boomhouse Haarlem, Getty Images (Alex
and Laila, American Images Inc, Burazin, George Diebold, English School, Dorling Kindersley,
John Lee, Sharon Montrose, Steve Morenos/Newspix, Joel Sartore, Vano Shlamov/AFP, Kim Taylor,
Gandee Vasan, Jerry Young), iStockphoto (Jill Battaglia, Eric Isselée, Andrey Khrolenok,
Valerie Loiseleux, William Allen Mole, Soren Pilman, Brian Weed, Eric Wong, Kenneth C. Zirkel)

Library of Congress Cataloging-in-Publication Data
Riggs, Ann.
Nouns and pronouns / by Ann Riggs.
p. cm. — (Understanding grammar)
Includes bibliographical references and index.
Summary: An examination of the rules behind English grammar, focusing on the components known
as nouns and pronouns, which name the people, places, and things that serve as the subjects and
objects of sentences.
ISBN 978-1-60818-093-6
1. English language—Noun. 2. English language—Pronoun. 3. English language—Grammar.
I. Title. II. Series.

PE1205.R54 2010
428.2—dc22 2010028301

CPSIA: 110310 PO1386

First Edition
2 4 6 8 9 7 5 3 1

TABLE of CONTENTS

Music swells. Siblings squabble. Owls hoot. I am. Grammar is.

And just like that, two words can become a SENTENCE. The information in a short sentence can be expanded by adding more words that give vivid descriptions or specific reactions. Where should those words be placed? How does a writer know what PUNCTUATION to use? What does all of that mean, anyway? Words fall into place more easily when one has an understanding of grammar, a system of rules that gives writers the foundation for producing acceptable, formal expression. It is that acceptable form, that appropriate grammar, which helps readers comprehend what has been written.

Look around you. What do you see, feel, taste, hear, or smell? All of your answers will fit into one category of grammatical identification: the noun. Our word "noun" is derived from the Latin word *nomen*, meaning "name." When Roman armies journeyed over land and sea from 75 B.C. through the first century A.D. they spread their language far and wide. Definitions of many other words have changed throughout the centuries, but the meaning of *noun* has not. It is still the *name* of something—a person, a thing, a place, a concept, or an idea.

Basic sentences have a subject (someone or something) and a PREDICATE or verb (action or state of being). Nouns are used in sentences as subjects or OBJECTS, and they can also rename those words and show possession, or ownership, of something. A noun may change its spelling to show different characteristics, such as singular or plural form (*apple/apples*). But if the same word is used over and over, saying that noun would become monotonous. To keep that from happening, another word can act as its substitute. That's what a pronoun (Latin *pro*, meaning "in place of") does. Pronouns can be used in place of nouns in all the ways nouns are used in sentences. And they have their own classifications and functions, too. Whether they name a person, place, or thing, nouns and pronouns provide the reasons for writing sentences in the first place—they're the topics of discussion.

NOUNS FOR ALL REASONS

Classifying nouns gives us many categories and ways to identify them in sentences. The two basic types of nouns are common and proper. A common noun starts with a lowercase letter as in "brother," unless it begins a sentence or appears in a title, such as "Band of Brothers." A proper noun is a name for a specific noun and always begins with a capital letter, no matter where it occurs in a sentence. See Table 1 for a comparison of some common and proper nouns.

Common nouns can also be classified as being concrete or abstract. Concrete nouns physically exist; they are visible and touchable. Whatever you're sitting on, looking at, or writing with, as well as other people who are nearby, these are all concrete nouns. Such nouns may be identified as count nouns because they can be counted one by one to get a total and because they have singular and plural forms, as in *chair/chairs*, *pen/pens*, *student/students*. Some concrete nouns are known as mass nouns because they are viewed as a quantity, or a mass, rather than as individual parts. Mass nouns—such as *food*, *homework*, and *sand*—have no precise shape or boundary and no one-word meaning, but they may be measured by count nouns: *boxes of food*, *pages of homework*, *buckets of sand*.

Not all count and mass nouns are concrete, though. Abstract nouns can't be physically touched; they're just ideas, or particular features, feelings, and concepts represented by words such as *cowardice*, *respect*, and *greed*. Those are examples of abstract mass nouns that are used only in singular form. Other abstract nouns are countable, such as *goal/goals*, *belief/beliefs*, and *freedom/freedoms*. Still another category of common nouns is the collective noun, which names a group: *tribe*, *flock*, or *assembly*. And finally, we have the compound, a noun that consists of more than one word and sometimes uses hyphens: *passerby*, *sister-in-law*, and *right of way*.

With so many categories and possibilities, is it any wonder that nouns decisively affect the sentences we write? Remember that a sentence requires both a subject and a verb; we need a *doer* and something for it to *do*, unless the subject is just existing, which verbs can also *do*. But the subject—the theme of the sentence—demands careful consideration, because it's essential that readers know what we're talking about.

French author Victor Hugo (1802–85) wrote his historical novel *Ninety-three* (1874) about a COUNTERREVOLUTIONARY revolt in 1793 France. Twenty common nouns are part of the following excerpt describing just one weapon, a ship's cannon. Can you find all the nouns?

COMMON NOUN	PROPER NOUN
author	Mark Twain
building	Empire State Building
cookie	Oreo
city	San Francisco
dog	Snoopy
month	February
ocean	Atlantic Ocean
school	Harvard University
vehicle	Jeep
war	World War I

TABLE 1

" The mad mass has the bounds of a panther, the weight of the elephant, the agility of the mouse, the obstinacy of the axe, the unexpectedness of the surge, the rapidity of lightning, the deafness of the tomb. It weighs ten thousand pounds, and it rebounds like a child's ball. Its flight is a wild whirl abruptly cut at right angles. "

Of the 20 nouns, only 2—*mass* and *flight*—are used as subjects. We can determine how the other 18 are used by examining their case, one of the four PROPERTIES of nouns. Case refers to the connection one word has to the others in a sentence. The English language has three cases: nominative, objective, and possessive. The nominative case, meaning "related to naming," identifies the required subject, as well as a predicate nominative (also known as a predicate noun), if there is one. In Hugo's last sentence, **Its flight is a wild whirl abruptly cut at right angles**, the LINKING VERB *is* leads to the predicate nominative *whirl*. Predicate nouns such as *whirl* can be identified by saying the subject (flight), the word "equals," and the noun after the linking verb. So, *flight = whirl* shows that both nouns are in the nominative case.

Determining the case of a noun may be a matter of distinguishing a subject in nominative case from an object, a noun in the objective case. Hugo's description of the military cannon uses a series of seven nouns as direct objects (nouns that follow action verbs) in the first sentence. Asking, "Mass has what?" returns the answers *bounds, weight, agility, obstinacy, unexpectedness, rapidity,* and *deafness*. These nouns are objects of the verb *has*, related to the subject *mass*. What's more, each object is followed by a PREPOSITIONAL PHRASE with another noun as the OBJECT OF THE PREPOSITION *of*. Both verbs and prepositions can have objects to complete their connections to other words in a sentence. If all the nouns were taken out of Hugo's description, what would the effect be?

> The mad _ has the _ of a _, the _ of the _, the _ of the _, the _ of the _, the _ of the _, the _ of _, the _ of the _. It weighs ten thousand _, and it rebounds like a child's _. Its _ is a wild _ abruptly cut at right _.

The words that stand out now are **a** and **the**, which are called articles. These words provide big clues to identifying the nouns in a sentence because, like a road sign, they point to the noun that's coming. Another article, **an**, is used before nouns that begin with a vowel (a, e, i, o, u) or a vowel sound, such as the silent *h* in *an honor* or *an hour*.

Words that directly follow another noun, renaming it and giving more information about it, are called appositives. The case of an appositive is the same case as the noun preceding it. A word such as "sister," when used after a person's name, can be an appositive. A person's name can also be an appositive if that name appears after "sister." For examples of appositives, take a look at the following excerpt from *The Hiding Place* (1971), by Dutch author Corrie ten Boom (1892–1983). She describes a time in her life when her aunts—named Jans, Bep, and Anna—were part of her overcrowded, extended family of nine.

" Tante [Aunt] Jans, Mama's older sister, had moved in with us when her husband died to spend, as she put it, "what few days remain to me," though she was still only in her early forties.

Her coming had greatly complicated life in the old house—already crowded by the earlier arrivals of Mama's other two sisters, Tante Bep and Tante Anna. "

Sister is an appositive to *Tante Jans,* the subject, in the first sentence. Because it follows (and helps identify) the subject, *sister* is in the nominative case. In the last sentence, it's the other way around; *Tante Bep* and *Tante Anna* are appositives to *sisters*. They give additional information about the object *sisters* by supplying their names. Because *sisters* is the object of the preposition *of,* it is in the objective case, and so are the appositives.

The third case, besides nominative and objective, is possessive. We use the possessive case with nouns to show ownership. In the excerpt on page 10, an apostrophe and an *-s* show possession in the phrase **Mama's older sister.** Tante Jans belongs to Mama as her "older sister," and thus *Mama's* is in the possessive case.

FLIGHT = WHIRL

BUILD YOUR OWN SENTENCE
It's Common Knowledge

Since all the things, places, people, ideas, and concepts you can think of are nouns, it should be easy to use at least 25 of them to write a paragraph. Jog your memory of a field trip to a museum or another historical exhibit by looking up pictures of the site online or in books. Now write about it. Your topic may involve a proper noun—a person—who helped explain the displays to you, or it may be about an artifact you found particularly intriguing. Perhaps your favorite memory of the trip comes from the bus ride or your lunch break! See how easy it is to incorporate so many nouns into your writing.

PROPERTY MANAGEMENT

A sentence's nominative case subject must agree with its verb in number, the second property of nouns. This means that if a singular count noun is the subject of a sentence, it will need a singular verb, such as **The *announcer has* a pleasing voice.** Likewise, if a plural count noun is the subject, it will need a plural verb. A mass noun is usually considered singular in number and will have a singular verb form, as in ***Silence is* golden.** A collective noun, though, can go either way, depending on its meaning. When being considered as a group of one singular amount, use a singular verb, as in ***Five dollars is* the price of the ticket.** But when the collective noun means a group of separate items, use a plural verb, such as ***Dollars are exchanged* for euro in France.**

Most plurals are formed by adding *-s* or *-es* to the singular form of a noun, such as *star/ stars*. When the singular form of a noun ends in *-ch*, *-s*, *-sh*, *-x* or *-z*, an *-es* is used to form the plural: *bench/benches*, *moss/mosses*, *bush/ bushes*, *toolbox/toolboxes*, and *waltz/waltzes*. Forming the plural of other nouns that have special spelling rules presents even further challenges. When in doubt, always look up the word in a dictionary.

The trick to forming the plural of a compound noun (consisting of more than one word) is deciding what part is the true noun. Compound nouns are made up of a modifier—a

for breakfast. Two singular nouns joined by *and* make the complete subject plural, so the verb must also be plural: **Bill *and* Sandy *are* shooting baskets in the gym.** When two plural nouns are joined by *and,* the subject is still plural, and the verb also needs to be plural, as in **Blue jays *and* song sparrows *are seen* in this region.** However, deciding whether to use a singular or plural verb in a complete subject that has both a singular noun (one word or a compound) and a plural noun joined by *or* depends on which part of the subject is closer to the verb. In the sentence **A rose *or* daffodils *are* often the centerpiece,** "daffodils" is a plural noun and

word that describes or qualifies a noun—and a noun. In order to make the plural of the compound mean "more than one," add -*s* to the noun, as in brother-in-law/*brothers*-in-law, runner-up/*runners*-up, and maid of honor/*maids* of honor.

When two singular nouns are joined by *or,* the COMPLETE SUBJECT is still singular (after all, it's just one *or* the other) and needs a singular verb: **An egg *or* cereal *is* all Roger eats**

is closer to the verb (are), so the verb is plural. If the subjects were in the opposite order, the verb would be singular.

A good rule of thumb when trying to make a complete subject agree with its verb is to look for the noun that is closer to the verb and match singular with singular, plural with plural, in spite of how it may sound to you. Also avoid being distracted by other words in the sentence that may be added to the complete subject, as in this sentence: **Rusty, as well as all the other team members, *is going* to the tournament.** The singular verb, *is going*, agrees with the singular subject, *Rusty*, despite the phrase that separates them. In the next example, the plural subject (*daughters*) matches the plural verb (*are going*): **All five *daughters*, as well as their dad, *are going* to the game.**

Did you notice that most of the plural nouns end in the letter -*s*? No plural noun is formed with an apostrophe. Using '*s* only shows possession, not a change from singular to plural. All possessive case singular nouns, even those that end in -*s*, from *architect's* to *James's*, use '*s*. But the possessive of a plural noun that ends in -*s* or -*es* is formed by adding only an apostrophe: **twelve *eggs'* shells, both *counties'* roads**, and **the *Joneses'* yard.** If the plural doesn't end in -*s*, add '*s*: ***men's* responsibilities, *geese's* ponds**, or ***alumni's* tables.** And if the plural involves a compound noun, add '*s* to the last word of the compound form: ***brothers-in-law's* tuxedos, *rights-***

STUDENTS, YOU MAY BEGIN

of-way's **confusion**, and *maids of honor's* **dresses.** Never use an apostrophe to make the plural of a name, though—unless you also want to show that the people own something.

Nouns may sometimes be people, but the "person" of a noun refers to the relationship between the noun and the speaker in a sentence. The characteristic that shows that the noun is speaking, denoting first person, is shown in this sentence: **We *teachers* will assign grades.** When the noun is being spoken to, in the second person, it may be expressed this way: ***Students,* you may begin.** And when the noun is being spoken about, in the third person, it can look like this: **The *teacher* gives the test.**

Nouns can also have gender, which is the last of the properties. A masculine noun (*man, king,* or *nephew*) shows that the subject, predicate nominative, or object of a sentence is male. Feminine designations include *woman, queen,* and *niece.* Neutral or neuter nouns are not specific to one gender or include both male and female, as in *human being, royalty,* and *family.* Sometimes only the suffix, or word ending, is changed to show a noun's gender, such as *actor/actress, waiter/waitress,* and *executor/executrix.* Compound nouns may also be gender specific: *boyfriend, gentlemen,* and *daughter-in-law.* But in general, there is no distinction

among masculine, feminine, and neuter in most English nouns. Think of *animals, couches,* and *gymnasiums,* for instance.

To summarize all the properties of nouns (case, number, person, and gender), we can turn to one of literature's most famous figures. In 1843, English writer Charles Dickens (1812–70) wrote his classic tale, *A Christmas Carol.* Dickens immortalized the character of Ebenezer Scrooge, whose name became synonymous not only with greed but also with redemption. Look for Dickens's assortment of nouns in the following passage that describes Scrooge and his determination to have business run as usual, even on the day of his partner Jacob Marley's burial.

Charles Dickens, pictured in the 1860s

" Marley was dead.... There is no doubt whatever about that. The register of his burial was signed by the clergyman, the clerk, the undertaker, and the chief mourner. Scrooge signed it: and Scrooge's name was good upon 'Change [where merchants met to do business], for anything he chose to put his hand to. Old Marley was as dead as a door-nail....

Scrooge knew he was dead? Of course he did. How could it be otherwise? Scrooge and he were partners for I don't know how many years. Scrooge was his sole executor, his sole administrator, his sole assign [person appointed to act on another's behalf], his sole residuary legatee [heir], his sole friend and sole mourner. And even Scrooge was not so dreadfully cut up [distressed] by the sad event, but that he was an excellent man of business on the very day of the funeral, and solemnised it with an undoubted bargain. "

Dickens provides us with a chance to see all four properties at work, as well as both common and proper nouns. The two proper nouns, Scrooge and Marley, identify the principal characters discussed in this passage; the rest of the nouns are common. Furthermore, each of the five sentences in the first paragraph has a singular, third-person noun subject in the nominative case that agrees with a singular verb: 1) *Marley was*, 2) *doubt is*, 3) *register was signed*, 4) *Scrooge signed*, and 5) *Marley was*. The third sentence, **The register of his burial was signed by the clergyman, the clerk, the undertaker, and the chief mourner,** has five objective case objects of prepositions. First is the preposition, *of*, and its common noun object, *burial*. After the verb is the preposition *by* and its series of four objects: *clergyman, clerk, undertaker,* and *mourner*. What's more, *clergyman* is a masculine noun— one of three used in the excerpt. And the possessive case use of *Scrooge's name* in the next sentence shows ownership.

In sentence four of the second paragraph, the plural COMPOUND SUBJECT, *Scrooge and he* [Marley], agrees with the plural verb, *were*, and is followed by a plural predicate nominative (or a noun that renames the subject in the predicate part of the sentence), *partners*. Renaming "Scrooge" six times in the next sentence are other predicate nominatives: *executor, administrator, assign, legatee, friend,* and *mourner*. What about the final sentence of

ON THE DAY OF THE FUNERAL

the excerpt? It has five objective case objects of prepositions: **by the *event*, of *business*, on the *day*, of the *funeral*,** and **with *bargain*.** But some sentences have subjects, objects, and words showing possession that aren't nouns. What are these words called?

BUILD YOUR OWN SENTENCE
What Did You Learn Today?

 Some people think that children should begin their formal education at a very early age and spend most of their time on school studies. Others believe that young children should spend most of their time playing. What do you think? Perhaps your opinion is formed from your adventures in preschool—or from your having learned at

home until you were old enough to go to kindergarten or first grade. Consider your earliest educational experiences and write about them, making a choice between the two schools of thought. People's names will give you a chance to practice correct apostrophe usage when naming a teacher's classroom or perhaps a friend's toy you shared; focus, as well, on correct subject-verb agreement and appropriately spelled plurals.

CALL IN THE SUBSTITUTES

Apronoun is a word that replaces, or substitutes for, a noun. Pronouns are used in sentences in the same ways as—and share the same four properties of—the nouns they rename. In addition, a pronoun must agree with its ANTECEDENT in person, number, and gender, taking its cue from the word or group of words it refers to, such as the antecedent, *Fran,* and the pronoun, *she,* in this sentence: **When *Fran* came to class late, *she* gave the teacher a note.** A singular noun has a singular pronoun to replace it; a plural noun has a plural pronoun substitute. Pronouns also have five classes that define their uses in sentences: personal, demonstrative, interrogative, relative, and indefinite.

Personal pronouns comprise the largest of the five classes, since they are used as substitutes for all common and proper nouns with a definite person or thing as an antecedent. Personal refers to the "person" of the speaker. A first-person speaker uses personal pronouns such as *I* and *my*, as in **I want the book to be sent to *my* home address.** When the pronoun is second person, it is being spoken to, such as ***You* will have plenty of time to finish.** Third person refers to a noun previously mentioned: **The Morrisons got *their* dog from the animal shelter.** The pronoun *their* refers to Morrisons, the name of the people being talked about. While personal pronouns also have number, case, and gender—just like nouns—third-person singular personal pronouns are the only ones that reflect gender: masculine {*he, him, his*}, feminine {*she, her, hers*}, and neuter or neutral {*it, its*}.

The masculine third-person pronouns have traditionally been used to refer to men or women when the antecedent's gender is not specified, as in this sentence: **The pharmacist serves all of *his* customers.** We don't know if the pharmacist is a man or a woman, but grammatically, it doesn't make a difference. Some writers prefer to alternate between masculine and feminine pronouns to give equal representation and avoid offending readers when the noun's gender cannot be determined. Using the

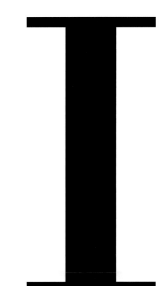

plural *their*, even in singular references, has never been grammatically correct, but it may be acceptable in informal writing. Saying, ***Everyone* must do *their* own assignment,** is sometimes an allowable substitute for the awkward ***Everyone* must do *his/her* own assignment,** even though the pronoun *everyone* is singular, and the possessive pronoun *their* is plural, toppling our concept of agreement between singular pronouns and their antecedents.

Consider this humorous tale of a misfit family of bullies, the Herdmans, from *The Best Christmas Pageant Ever* (1972), by Barbara Robinson (1927–). As you read, aim to identify the pronouns that are taking the place of nouns.

" They were really interested in Herod, and I figured they liked him. He was so mean he could have been their ancestor—Herod Herdman. But I was wrong.

"Who's going to be Herod in this play?" Leroy said.

"We don't show Herod in our pageant," Mother said. And they all got mad. They wanted somebody to be Herod so they could beat up on him.

I couldn't understand the Herdmans. You would have thought the Christmas story came right out of the F. B. I. files, they got so involved in it—wanted a bloody end to Herod, worried about Mary having her baby in a barn, and called the Wise Men a bunch of dirty spies.

And they left the first rehearsal arguing about whether Joseph should have set fire to the inn, or just chased the innkeeper into the next county.

THEY

HIS

How would parts of the opposite passage read if *Herod* and *the Herdmans* were used instead of the pronouns that referred to them?

> The Herdmans were really interested in Herod, and I figured the Herdmans liked Herod. Herod was so mean Herod could have been the Herdmans' ancestor—Herod Herdman. But I was wrong.... And the Herdmans all got mad. The Herdmans wanted somebody to be Herod so the Herdmans could beat up on Herod.

Both versions tell the same story, but the author's use of pronouns avoids needless repetition of the nouns and moves the story along. Once you know who Herod and the Herdmans are, the pronouns that come after their noun antecedents make perfect sense. In this segment, "they" clearly means the Herdmans: **I couldn't understand the Herdmans. You would have thought the Christmas story came right out of the F. B. I. files,** *they* **got so involved in it...**

BUILD YOUR OWN SENTENCE
Before and After

When we use a pronoun, its meaning should be obvious. That means the pronoun needs to rename whatever noun it refers to—its antecedent—and agree with it in number. Sometimes gender references stump us. Think about ways to say this sentence without using a masculine or feminine pronoun: "A student should hand in his/her papers promptly." Now rewrite the sentence four times, keeping the same basic meaning while making these changes: 1) Take out both pronouns. 2) Change the singular references to plural. 3) Begin the sentence with "Papers are to be…" and leave pronouns out. 4) Make the sentence a command and use second person (your).

ANSWER KEY

1) A student should hand in papers promptly. 2) Students should hand in their papers promptly. Or: Students should hand in papers promptly. 3) Papers are to be handed in promptly. 4) Hand in your papers promptly.

BUILDING A STRONG CASE

We've learned that pronouns must agree with their antecedents in person, number, and gender. But how can a writer tell which pronoun to use? Determining its function in the sentence and recognizing where it is placed is the key to solving the *case*. A personal pronoun used as a subject or predicate nominative will be in the nominative case {*I, we, you, he, she, it, they*}. For example, ***It*** (subject) **was *she*** (predicate nominative) **who voted to close the store.** Objective case pronouns {*me, us, you, him, her, it, them*} are correctly used as objects—direct, indirect, and objects of prepositions. Only possessive pronouns like the following show ownership: *my, mine, our, ours, your, yours, his, her, hers, its, their, theirs*. The following sentences illustrate all three cases: ***He*** (nominative-subject) **ordered a cheeseburger. The waitress gave *him*** (objective-indirect object) **the cheeseburger. The cheeseburger was *his*** (possessive). When a pronoun and its noun appositive are combined, choose the case of the pronoun as if the noun were not there, such as **In spite of the road conditions, the bus driver**

managed to get all of us *students* to school on time. The object of the preposition is "us." But this example uses nominative case: ***We students* are responsible.** In this case, the subject is "we."

Did you notice in the list above that the possessive pronouns do not have apostrophes? Unlike possessive case nouns, possessive personal pronouns never need an apostrophe. This sometimes confuses people if they are uncertain about how the pronoun functions within the sentence or if the pronoun sounds like another word that does have an apostrophe—a CONTRACTION. For instance, if you're looking for some friends who have left the room, you might say, ***They're* not over *there* in *their* seats anymore.** Okay, so maybe you wouldn't make such a confusing statement, but it does identify three HOMONYMS. The seats are *theirs*—they belong to them, but resist the temptation to add an apostrophe. The place, *there*, is complete in itself. Although the contraction *they're* has an apostrophe, it isn't possessive; the subject and verb are connected. The apostrophe merely shows that something is

THERE

missing—the letter *a* of the verb *are*.

How do you know when to use the possessive form *whose* and the contraction *who's*? First, remember that the possessive form of this word never needs an apostrophe. We can rephrase the question **Whose books are these?** this way: **The books are *whose*?** Then we can check ourselves by substituting another possessive pronoun in the answer, "The books are *his*." The fact that we can exchange *whose* for another possessive pronoun and maintain a grammatically correct sentence proves *whose* is correct. How does the other homonym differ? **Who's driving us home after practice tonight?** The contraction *who's* stands for the nominative subject *who* and the verb *is*. If we tried to use *whose* instead of the contraction, the sentence wouldn't have a subject and a verb: **Whose driving us home after practice tonight?** Someone should be *driving*—but *who is*?

This brings us to another stickler: *its* or *it's*. One of the two is a possessive pronoun (*its*). The other is a contraction for the two words *it is* (*it's*). The apostrophe makes it possible to leave out the *i* from *is*. *It's* confusing only if you don't know *its* meaning. The remedy? Try saying *it is* each time you want to use either one. Only

when the pronoun plus the verb makes sense will you correctly choose *it's*. So, *it is* confusing only if you don't know *it is* meaning? No, only the first *it is* qualifies as a contraction needing an apostrophe; the second *its* owns the right

to be without one. And if you're ever tempted to use an apostrophe in any other possessive pronoun, try adding *is*, as shown in the b) column on page 33.

One minor detail separates *your*, the

THEY'RE
THEIR

possessive pronoun, and *you're*, the nominative pronoun contraction that means *you are*. The contraction doesn't mean *your are*; the apostrophe simply stands for the omitted *a*. There is still no reason to ever put an apostrophe in the possessive pronouns *your* or *yours*. *You're* in control of *you* and *your*; it's all *yours*!

Because pronouns are like nouns when it comes to subject-verb agreement, a plural pronoun (*we, you, they*) pairs with a plural verb. While a singular pronoun (*I, he, she, it*) pairs with a singular verb, remember that verbs ending in *-s* are singular. Say **he was, she has,** and **it does.** Correct plural forms are **you were, they have, they do,** and **we don't.** The pronoun *you* always takes the plural verb form, even if *you* means second-person singular. That is why *you was* is never correct. You see, it really *does* matter, and saying that *it don't* is *not* right.

When a mix of nouns and pronouns or two pronouns compose a compound subject, the pronoun or noun nearer to the verb determines agreement. Here is a singular example: **The guys or *he chooses* the uniforms.** Now here's a plural one: **He or the *managers choose* the team mascot.** Additionally, if both pronouns or nouns are singular, the verb will also be singular: ***The coach or Jeremy has* the team roster.**

Objective case compounds also need careful study. The prepositional phrase "between you and me" is often incorrectly written "between you and I." The preposition *between* needs to be followed by objective case pronouns, such as *me, us, you, her, him, it,* or *them*. The pronoun *you* is correct in both nominative and objective uses, so the focus is on the other half of the compound, *I*. Recognizing that *I* is a subject—not an object—helps resolve the issue. Just between *us*, two objects of any preposition can be between you and *me*.

Personally Responsible

English playwright William Shakespeare's (1564–1616) *Julius Caesar* (1599) includes a famous funeral tribute by Caesar's friend, Marc Antony. Copy the speech onto paper as it is. Then make a list of the 14 italicized personal pronouns and their cases (nominative, objective, or possessive) as used below:

Friends, Romans, countrymen, lend *me*
　your ears.
I come to bury Caesar, not to praise *him*.
The evil that men do lives after *them*;
The good is oft interrèd with *their* bones.
So let *it* be with Caesar. The noble Brutus
Hath told *you* Caesar was ambitious.
If *it* were so, *it* was a grievous fault,
And grievously hath Caesar answered
　it....
He was *my* friend, faithful and just to *me*.

ANSWER KEY

me—objective, your—possessive, I—nominative, him—objective, them—objective, their—possessive, it—objective, you—objective, it—nominative, it—nominative, it—objective, he—nominative, my—possessive, me—objective.

MORE PRONOUNS WITH CLASS

The other four pronoun classes—demonstrative, interrogative, relative, and indefinite—do not have cases like personal pronouns do, but each comes with its own set of considerations. The demonstrative pronoun shows the way to its antecedent, using singular pronouns (*this* or *that*) and plural pronouns (*these* or *those*). Saying, **That is fantastic!** is an enthusiastic response to a friend's having told you about his new job. But if someone asks you if your clothes should be put in the garage sale pile, you may reply, **I want to keep *these.*** An interrogative pronoun (*what, which, who, whom*) begins a sentence that asks a question: **What was the assignment?** or **Who told you?**

Relative pronouns (*that, what, which, who, whom, whoever, whose*) help connect the part of a sentence that can stand alone with the part that is dependent. These pronouns may look like demonstratives or interrogatives, but when they are relating two parts of a sentence, they function as relative pronouns. **The library didn't have the book *that* I wanted.** The relative pronoun *that* refers to the noun "book" in the MAIN CLAUSE. **The lady *who* lives next door has a new dog.** The dependent clause, or the clause that depends upon the main clause for its meaning, "*who* lives next door" is related to "lady."

Indefinite pronouns (*all, another, any, anyone, both, each, either, everybody, everyone,*

few, *many*, *neither*, *nobody*, *none*, *no one*, *several*, *somebody*) do not substitute for specific nouns; they function as nouns themselves: ***Anybody* could have done it, but *nobody* volunteered. *All* are welcome. *Everyone* is expected to arrive on time.** In that last example, "*everyone* is" shows the correct agreement between the singular subject and verb.

American playwright Moss Hart (1904–61) uses examples of each pronoun class in the following excerpt from his autobiography, *Act One* (1959). Growing up in Manhattan and feeling excluded by his tough, athletic peers, Hart recalls how his interest in reading gained him recognition and changed his status from that of an outsider's.

ALL
ANOTHER
ANY
ANYONE
BOTH
EACH
EITHER
EVERYONE
MANY
NEITHER
NONE

" I can no longer remember which boy it was that summer evening who broke the silence with a question; but whoever he was, I nod to him in gratitude now. "What's in those books you're always reading?" he asked idly. "Stories," I answered. "What kind?" asked somebody else without much interest.

Nor do I know what impelled me to behave as I did, for usually I just sat there in silence, glad enough to be allowed to remain among them; but instead of answering his question, I launched full tilt into the book I was immersed in at the moment.... They listened bug-eyed and breathless. I must have told it well, but I think there was another and deeper reason that made them so flattering an audience. Listening to a tale being told in the dark is one of the most ancient of man's entertainments, but I was offering them as well, without being aware of doing it, a new and exciting experience. The books they themselves read were the *Rover Boys* or *Tom Swift* or G. A. Henty. I had read them too, but at thirteen I had long since left them behind. "

THEY
LISTENED

The excerpt begins with the first-person pronoun *I* used as the subject (**I can no longer remember**) and draws the reader to the third-person nominative subject *he* **asked idly** in the next sentence. The third-person plural nominative subject (**They listened**) in the second paragraph stands for the same boys in the last paragraph; *they* reappears with the added emphasis of the third-person plural pronoun *themselves* in **books *they* themselves read.**

In the second and last paragraphs, Hart also uses objective case personal pronouns. These three are direct objects: **what impelled *me*, told *it* well**, and **left *them* behind.** And the last one is an object of a preposition: **to remain among *them*.** An example of

possessive case is in the first sentence of the second paragraph when the author says, **instead of answering *his* question.** This third-person singular, masculine gender pronoun gives ownership to a boy who asked about the books Hart had read.

In the first sentence of the excerpt, a demonstrative pronoun points to the specific night of the event by stating ***that* summer evening,** while the interrogative pronouns that follow lead to the questions ***What's (what is)* in those books?** and ***What* kind?** A refresher course in the importance of relative pronouns can be found in the four times the author relates dependent clauses to the main parts of their sentences: ***who* broke the silence, *whoever* he was, *which* boy it was,** and

that made them so flattering an audience. The short excerpt even includes two indefinite pronouns: **asked** *somebody* **else** and **there was** *another* **and deeper reason.**

Sometimes, because of their function in the sentence, demonstrative and indefinite pronouns serve as adjectives and are then called PRONOMINAL ADJECTIVES; they modify nouns and other pronouns. In the excerpt above, *that* **summer evening** employs the demonstrative pronoun *that* to describe the noun "evening," and **there was** *another* **and deeper reason** uses the indefinite pronoun *another* to modify "reason." Many pronouns can function as adjectives, but they are still considered pronouns.

Why are nouns so important to us? They're the first words we learn as infants and toddlers: **"Mama!" "Dada!"** What's more, nouns remain prominent as we further explain the world around us, and that importance doesn't diminish as our vocabulary grows. Good writers know that specific nouns help keep readers interested and that precise pronouns avoid stilted, monotonous noun repetition. While there are many ways to define and use nouns and pronouns, without them we wouldn't have complete sentences or diverse word choices for the same people, places, things, ideas, and concepts. Nouns continue to be the basis for why writers write, so we must learn their names and use them well!

MAMA!
DADA!
MAMA!
DADA!
MAMA!
DADA!

BUILD YOUR OWN SENTENCE
Of Relative Importance

People often fondly remember presents that they have received, and often the person giving it was more special than the object. Write about a gift you were given that has particular meaning for you. Perhaps the item was your uncle's, your grandfather's, or your mom's possession first and then was handed down to you. Use appropriate relative, demonstrative, indefinite, and interrogative pronouns to show the *what* and *who* about *this* gift, as well as whether *everyone* else you know also has one like it. *Why* is it special to you? If you need help, refer to pages 36 and 37 for more information about the pronoun types.

GLOSSARY

antecedent: a word or group of words that comes before a pronoun and that the pronoun refers to

complete subject: the part of a sentence that contains a noun or pronoun and any modifiers that describe it and help complete the meaning of the subject

compound subject: two or more subjects using the same verb in a sentence

contraction: a shortened form of a word or group of words, with the missing letters usually marked by an apostrophe

counterrevolutionary: opposed to a rebellion

homonyms: words that sound alike but have different meanings and spellings

linking verb: a verb that does not have action; it joins the subject to its complement

main clause: a group of words with a subject and a verb that makes sense by itself and to which other dependent clauses may be connected

object of the preposition: a noun or pronoun that a preposition (*at, by, of, to,* etc.) relates to another word or word group

objects: people or things to which a specified action is directed

predicate: the part of a clause or sentence containing a verb and stating something about the subject

prepositional phrase: a group of words consisting of a preposition (*at, by, of, to,* etc.), its object, and any modifiers

pronominal adjectives: pronouns that function like adjectives to describe a noun

properties: characteristics and qualities of a word or group of words

punctuation: marks used to provide meaning and separate elements within sentences, such as periods, commas, question marks, exclamation points, semicolons, colons, hyphens, and parentheses

sentence: a unit of expression that contains a subject and a verb and expresses a complete, independent thought

SELECTED BIBLIOGRAPHY

The Chicago Manual of Style. 15th ed. Chicago: The University of Chicago Press, 2003.

Darling, Charles. "Guide to Grammar." Capital Community College Foundation. http://grammar.ccc.commnet.edu/grammar/.

Hodges, John C., Winifred B. Horner, Suzanne S. Webb, and Robert K. Miller. *Harbrace College Handbook*. 13th ed. Fort Worth, Tex.: Harcourt Brace College Publishers, 1998.

Hunter, Estelle B., ed. *The New Self-Teaching Course in Practical English and Effective Speech*. Chicago: The Better-Speech Institute of America, 1935.

Lederer, Richard, and Richard Dowis. *Sleeping Dogs Don't Lay: Practical Advice for the Grammatically Challenged*. New York: St. Martin's Press, 1999.

O'Connor, Patricia T. *Woe Is I Jr.: The Younger Grammarphobe's Guide to Better English*. New York: G. P. Putnam's Sons, 2007.

Strunk, William, and E. B. White. *The Elements of Style*. 4th ed. New York: Longman Publishers, 2000.

Warriner, John E., Joseph Mersand, and Francis Griffith. *English Grammar and Composition*. New York: Harcourt, Brace & World, Inc, 1963.

INDEX